How to Start Gardening

Also by Fran Barnwell

The New to Gardening series:

How to Start Gardening: A Step by Step Guide for Beginners (2nd edition)

How to Grow Orchids: A Beginner's Guide to Growing Orchids

How to Start
Gardening

A Step by Step Guide
for Beginners

by
Fran Barnwell

Published by: Rowan House Publishing

First Printing, 2012

Liability disclaimer

By reading this book, you assume all risks associated with using the advice given below, with a full understanding that you, solely, are responsible for anything that may occur as a result of putting this information into action in any way, and regardless of your interpretation of the advice.

Clematis: 'Wm Kennett' and 'The President'

Table of Contents

Preface to the Second Edition

Since writing this book in 2005, much has changed, not only in my life but in gardening in general. There has been a trend, and a welcome one on my part, more towards organic gardening and gardening for the benefit of wildlife: a trend that has been echoed in farming circles as well.

For that reason, I felt I had to update this book. The basic information I give you here is still relevant, although I have 'tweaked' here and there as more experience has taught me better, easier or quicker ways to do things. For example, I have added a new section on collecting seeds from plants. This has been something that I have found exceptionally rewarding as well as an activity that anyone new to gardening can do.

In addition, I wanted to add a chapter on organic gardening. Although in the past I admit that I have resorted to chemical fertilisers and pest control, particularly when dealing with slugs, I wanted to find out just how difficult or not it would be for someone with limited time to be able to garden organically. This new chapter also looks at the dangers of continuing to use chemical fertilisers and the benefits of organic gardening as well as giving practical advice to help you get started.

And in this second edition, I have also added more photographs, in full colour, in addition to those taken in my own garden. I wanted to be able to show more examples of the plants and techniques discussed, and these photographers have been credited in the appropriate section at the back of the book.

FRAN BARNWELL

Introduction

I have written this book because I know from experience how it feels to look at your brand new garden and wonder 'where on earth do I start?' or 'what do I have to do first?'

And I found that although there were many books on gardening, somehow I felt that the experts had forgotten what it was like to be a beginner. There seemed to be so many rules –gardening has to be done in a certain way, and you must have the exact equipment – it all becomes so perplexing, that you end up not doing anything rather than doing something and getting it wrong. So I wanted to tell you about my experiences and what I have learned, to prove to you that you can achieve something really worthwhile and feel pride in that achievement, and that it's not, in fact, that difficult at all.

First of all, a little bit about me. I have always loved the garden, having been given a little patch of my own to tend when I was a child. But as an adult, I had little opportunity to carry on gardening until I moved to my present home in Cornwall, in south-west England, in 1999. This was my first home with a garden. My knowledge was very limited, having forgotten most of what I had learned from my mother. But I was determined to have a garden that not only flowered for most of the year (I have the good fortune to live in a mild temperate climate), but one that would also accommodate my dogs, cats and guinea pigs. And that is what I have been able to do.

Wisteria, late April

I want to be able to show that you too, if you take those first steps, will have successes. Yes, you will also make some mistakes, although you will learn that for the most part they are recoverable, but most importantly, you will discover the fascination of gardening – that no two months or two years are ever the same.

This book was always intended to be the first in a series of books – under the title of The New to Gardening Series – to help the newbie gardener. It therefore gives the beginner the very basic information needed to get started. The chapters cover topics such as, the simple equipment needed, different types of plants, dealing with pests, how to grow your own plants from seed and a chapter on organic gardening.

Throughout this book I will be using common names for most of the plants with the Latin name in brackets, if these are different, to make it easier to identify the plants I'm talking about.

This is not a very large book, but that is because I don't want you to spend your time reading; I want you to spend your time out in the garden. I want you to be able to read through the step by step instructions and be able to put them straight into practice.

My aim is to motivate, inspire, and encourage you to begin gardening. Just get started, follow the advice and tips in this book, and remember that your plants do actually want to grow. And if after reading this book you take action, then I will feel that I have succeeded.

Camellia, 'Golden Spangles'

Chapter 1

What You Need to Know

Before you get started

I can understand that when you first take over your garden space, it is a very ex-
citing moment and you
are full of enthusiasm to
get started – whether you
have just bare soil, or a
garden full of established
plants. But before you
can get going you need to
make certain decisions if
your hard work and ef-
fort are not going to be
wasted. And this is a first step you have to go through if
you want your gardening to have a chance of success.

So you start off by asking yourself a few questions:

- How much spare time do you have that you can
  spend working in the garden?

- How much money do you have to spend on plants or landscaping?
- What size space do you have?
- And what do you want to achieve with the space you have? How do you want your garden to function?

This then leads on to further questions:

- Do you work full-time, and are your weekends filled with social activities, which can limit the amount of time you can spend on the garden?
- Are you happy to buy established plants from a nursery or do you want to grow your own plants from seed?
- Do you have dogs and cats who could damage your plants or do you need space for children's ballgames?

The answers to these questions will begin to give you an idea as to the purpose your garden has to serve, and give you a realistic picture of how much work you can put into the garden, and take into account any time or money constraints. And even if all you have is a balcony or small courtyard, or if you don't have too much spare cash, this is still no barrier to having a flowerful and productive space.

So let's now start to look at exactly what is involved in getting to grips with gardening and start with some basics.

What do plants need?

Very simply they need soil, water, light and warmth, and nutrients. All of these can be provided by the plants' natural environment, but when they are newly planted out in the garden or into containers, they need quite a bit of help from us and I'll get to that shortly.

And what do you need?

The basic tools are spade, fork, trowel, hand fork, watering can, and secateurs, and some green garden twine is useful. If you wish, you can add a rake, wheelbarrow and hoe. There is no need to spend a great amount on these, they can be found for a reasonable price in most garden centres, or ask parents and grandparents if they have any tools they no longer use.

In addition to the tools you need, I suggest that you invest in a good quality plant handbook, which ideally should give you the following information for each plant: how tall and wide it grows, and how fast, the type of soil the plant prefers; whether it likes sun or shade, dry or damp conditions; and the time of year it flowers. It is also extremely helpful if the book actually has photos of each of the plants (see Further Reading).

7

Make friends with the staff at your local plant nursery, who will welcome your questions and be happy to share their knowledge. If they don't have time for your questions – go elsewhere.

There is some technical 'stuff' that garden experts usually tell you is essential before you can create a successful garden. There is a great temptation to skip this part – and I know, because I have done it – but it is well worth that little bit of extra effort to understand what you need to know before getting started.

Soil type

The type of soil you have in your garden is important as it determines which plants will do well and which will struggle to grow. As a point of interest, this soil type is a result of the underlying bedrock and its constituents in your area.

Here are some clues to help you identify some of these differences:

- Clay soil – when it rains, clay soil becomes heavy, sticky mud, slow to drain away, but when dry, the soil becomes hard and forms cracks. In your hands, this soil is easily formed into a smooth solid ball.
- Chalky soil – you will often see small pieces of white chalk within the soil, which is usually fairly light in colour. It drains very quickly.

- Sandy soil – this type of soil feels gritty and is difficult to form a solid lump in your hands, and water will drain away very quickly.
- Loamy soil – this is the ideal soil for gardeners, dark brown, crumbly but can be formed into a ball. It holds water well but excess will drain away quickly.

In addition to this, your soil can be either acid or alkaline. You can buy a soil testing kit from your local garden centre, they're not expensive, and I believe they are quite easy to use.

The kit will tell you the pH of the soil based on the calcium content – a pH of 7 is neutral, and most plants will grow quite happily: higher than that is alkaline (higher in calcium) and lower than 7 is acid.

There are two different types of testing kits: one is the probe type, as illustrated above, where a probe is pushed into t he soil and the pH registers on the meter.

An alternative is to buy a kit which uses a chemical solution that, when mixed with a soil sample from your garden, changes colour. Matching the colour to those on the chart will give you the pH of the soil in that particular area of your garden. Whichever method you use, it is best to test different areas of your garden, as there may be some variation, for instance if you have deciduous trees, leaf litter can increase the acidity of the soil.

Gardening books often use different terms to mean the same thing, so plants that grow in acid soil, such as camellias and azaleas, are sometimes called 'acid lovers' or 'lime haters' – it's the same thing.

However, there is an even easier way: my own method of discovering the type of soil in my garden, was simply to have a good look at what plants were already growing in my own and neighbours' gardens. And ask questions; you will find that most people are delighted to tell you about their successes and what has not worked and, if you're lucky, may even offer to give you spare plants or cuttings.

And if you have taken over an established garden, you will be able to see what plants are looking healthy and those that are not. If you move into your house in winter, then it's a good idea to wait for a season to see what plants come up during spring and summer.

Once you have established the type of soil you have, you can then begin to decide what plants will grow best. And while I'm on the subject of soil, I here want to touch on the very important subject of…

Soil improvement

Garden compost

It is becoming more and more apparent that we now need to recycle as much as we can, and anyone with a garden has a head start and can make a great contribution in the form of making garden compost.

So what exactly is compost? Compost is the result of organic matter – such as leaves and grass clippings, vegetable and fruit scraps, straw and small plant stems – which, when combined and left for a period of time, breaks down into a crumbly soil-like texture.

Compost in its finished form is used as a mulch: it reduces water loss from the soil, reduces or prevents weed growth, and helps to keep the soil at a constant temperature.

To many novice gardeners, including myself in the early days, the subject of compost can be a little difficult to grasp but in fact it is quite simple, with just a few points to remember.

You need a compost bin, and the type you have may depend on your budget or the size of your garden. A purpose-built plastic bin purchased from a garden centre is not too expensive; you just fill up from the top and a few months later, you can take compost from a small hatch at the base. Alternatively, if you can wield a saw and some nails, you can make a wooden slatted enclosure, one metre square – or you can buy them ready made – and cover it with a piece of old carpet to keep the worst of the weather off.

If you have the space, you could have two bins and, once you have filled the first, that can then be left to break down, and you can start filling the second.

Plastic and wooden compost bins

What you can compost

All uncooked vegetable and fruit peelings, teabags, tea leaves and coffee grounds, well-crushed egg shells, spent flowers from the house. And from the garden: spent bedding plants, dead leaves, lawn mowings – mixed with some dryer materials, soft prunings, shredded paper, rabbit and guinea pig bedding. It is best to have everything chopped up as small as possible to speed up the process.

What NOT to compost

All meat products and bones, bread, cooked food, which will attract vermin, dog or cat waste, woody material, weeds, and anything that is non-biodegradable, for example, plastics.

And because you won't always feel like taking a trip to the compost heap when it's wet or cold or every time you peel vegetables, why not keep a lidded container by the back door? You can fill it up and then make the trip to the compost every couple of days.

Over a period of time – three months to one year, depending on conditions – all this matter will have broken down into lovely dark-brown crumbly compost, which you can fork into your beds and borders. It makes an excellent soil conditioner and can be used as surface mulch, helping conserve moisture and discourage weeds.

One point to note is that that if you have too much green material, say, in the form of grass clippings, the bin can become smelly and slimy. Just make sure that you mix in some drier materials, such as shredded paper.

You can also convert fallen leaves into wonderful compost. Rake up any leaves from your lawn – you may have to do this several times over the autumn – and collect them from the borders. Put them all into a black waste sack, sprinkle with water, put a few holes around the sack with a fork, tie the top, and leave it in a corner for about a year. What you end up with is known as leaf-mould, which is particularly good used as a mulch. Although leaf-mould has no particular nutritious value, it is invaluable for improving soil structure. It also increases water retention of the soil and so is ideal for use in containers and hanging baskets.

Fertiliser

Plants need food, just as you and I do, but in the form of nitrogen (N), phosphorus (P) and potassium (K) – and that's about as technical as I'm going to get. At first, I found the subject of fertilisers very confusing as there is an enormous range of fertilisers to choose from, offering differing proportions of these three ingredients to suit a wide variety of purposes – to combat mineral deficiencies, to boost root growth, or more flowers, and even for different species of plants.

If you are not ready to tackle organic gardening (and you can read more about this in Chapter 6), you can buy a general-purpose fertiliser, which has a balance of all three nutrients and is perfectly adequate for most situations. Use on the soil before planting and for feeding established plants.

For containers, you can buy fertiliser in pellet form – just pop four or five into each container or hanging basket, depending on the size, while you are planting up, and this gives enough nutrients for the plants for the whole of the summer season.

Preparing the ground

Containers

If you just have pots on a balcony or patio, or window boxes, this bit is easier. And there are so many varieties of containers to choose from in the garden centres, you really are spoiled for choice – from reasonably priced plastic tubs, which can be painted any colour you choose, terracotta clay pots, through to more expensive glazed pots, and even metal pots – whatever takes your fancy and your finances. Do remember though that clay pots dry out quickly in hot weather and these pots need watering more frequently than others.

You will need a multi-purpose compost (if you are concerned about environmental issues, you can now buy peat-free compost from most garden centres – but do ask), fertiliser pellets, and you can also buy water-retaining granules, which when mixed into the compost when you are planting up, can help to prevent the compost from drying out in hot sun.

When planting in containers, you must make sure that the plant has good drainage so as not to become waterlogged when it is very rainy. To prevent blocking the drainage hole in the base of the pot, put in a layer of broken crocks, or even small pieces of polystyrene, which is lighter if you have a big heavy pot, so that the water can drain away quickly. You can also stand the pot on pot feet, which keeps the pot off the ground, also helping the water to drain away.

Beds and borders

Initially, I wondered if I was using the right word, but eventually found out that the difference between a garden bed and a garden border is its location – a border generally runs along the edge of a garden, with a wall or hedge at its back, and a bed is usually in the centre and you can walk right around it.

Digging

Digging is something that most new gardeners wonder how much they have to do, but again it's not as tricky as you might think. Much depends on the state of the garden that you take over. If you are lucky, the previous occupier has kept the garden in reasonable shape, and all you have to do is remove weeds, turn the soil over with a fork and to incorporate organic matter (homemade compost) to improve the condition of the soil.

At the risk of sounding boring, soil improvement is one of the most important tasks a gardener can do, and the better the condition of the soil, the better your plants will grow and the more success you will have.

If, however, you feel that the soil looks compacted, or you want to completely re-vamp a border for new planting, then you can get out the spade and 'single dig' (specific instructions on this technique can be found in Appendix I).

If you are really unlucky, then your garden may have been left untended for years and is overgrown with weed 'monsters' (see Chapter 4 for examples). And if you are moving into a brand new house, then your garden could be filled with builders' rubble and not much else, even if it has been laid to lawn.

If your garden is badly overgrown, whatever else you do, **DON'T use a rotavator**, as this will chop up the weed roots and helps them to grow and multiply at an awesome rate. The best thing you can do is to chop back all the top growth, and use a weedkiller based on glyphosate (be sure to follow the instructions carefully and take all the recommended precautions).

Even if you want to garden without chemicals in the future, this is really the only practical solution as any alternatives, such as digging all the roots out, can take a couple of years.

If your house is brand new, then getting your garden into a reasonable planting condition may well be somewhat of a headache, and there are no easy answers:

- Get rid of as much of the rubble and rubbish as you can;
- Start to improve the soil by incorporating compost and digging it in;
- In the meantime, brighten up the garden with containers;
- If you can afford to, and are in a hurry, you can buy topsoil, have it delivered and spread it over your garden, and you're off to a flying start.

If, however, you inherit a ready-made garden, work around features that are already there such as trees or big shrubs – don't be in a hurry to cut them right down, they may turn out to be a blessing.

And now, we come on to the most exciting part of gardening – the actual plants...

Chapter 2

Plants

Types of plants

So that you can have interest and variety in your garden or on your balcony all year round, it is important to understand what the different types of plants are, their purpose, and when they are at their best.

Perennials

Perennial plants are those that technically live for more than two years. In practice, they will provide the backbone of the garden. Some plants, such as lupins, hardy geraniums and delphiniums, known as herbaceous perennials, die down in the autumn but grow again in the spring. Others are evergreen, which can provide some interest in the garden during winter. I have to own up to the fact that, at first, I was not aware that some plants die back for the winter, and happily started digging them out thinking that they had died completely – I lost a few good plants in my first year. So it does help to identify what plants you have and how they behave and this is where a good plant encyclopaedia is a must.

A garden in summer

Annuals

Annuals are plants that grow, flower and die in one season, and are usually thrown away after flowering. You will probably be familiar with sweet peas (*lathyrus odoratus*), surfinias, shown here, sunflowers (*helianthus*), and the bedding plants used in public parks and gardens. These  plants can be used to fill in gaps, give instant colour, are used in containers and hanging baskets, and are always readily available in garden centres during April and May.

Bulbs

Bulbs can be so useful in a garden – think of daffodils (*narcissus*) and crocus – and, once they have been planted, require very little further effort. Don't cut off the flower stalks or leaves after flowering and let them die down naturally to feed the bulb for the following year.

Trees and shrubs

To give height and structure, trees and shrubs have an important part to play when planning and planting a garden. Another enormous benefit is that once they have settled into their new home, they are generally trouble free and require little maintenance apart from occasional pruning (see more about this later). If you have room for a tree, then you are very lucky – so many new gardens these days are far too small, though if you talk to your local nursery, they will be able to recommend a tree suitable for a smaller space. Many shrubs, such as forsythia and lilac (*syringa*), are deciduous – losing their leaves each autumn – and others, holly (*ilex*) and camellias, are evergreen.

Herbs

Herbs are plants often neglected by new gardeners, but well worth considering, as not only are they edible, and provide a delightful fragrance in the garden, they are also easy to grow. One of the most familiar in gardens is, of course, lavender, and along with rosemary, thyme and sage, are very attractive to bees.

Grasses

I have included grasses because they are becoming increasingly popular in all types of garden. They can be either evergreen or herbaceous; they can be clump-forming acting as ground cover, or they can be gracefully statuesque adding real presence to a garden. They are also disease and pest resistant, making them ideal for those with minimal time to spend in the garden.

Styles of planting

You will discover that many plants cross boundaries between one type of planting and another, so, for instance, red-hot pokers (*kniphofia*) look good in both cottage gardens and prairie planting. Be bold with your planting – if you like the plant and it likes the conditions it will grow in, then go ahead and plant it.

Remember, there is no 'right' or 'wrong' way, and also remember that in nature, colour never clashes, so whatever colours you grow together will work. As I am writing this, I have bright yellow Welsh poppies (*mecanopsis cambrica*) flowering amongst magenta-coloured gladioli. You wouldn't necessarily put these two colours together, but you know what? They look just fine. Christopher Lloyd has been an inspiration for many gardeners in looking at colour in the garden from a different perspective (see Further Reading).

So what different styles of planting are there?

Cottage gardens

We are all familiar with the 'chocolate box' image of the cottage garden – masses of flowers, all prettily tumbling together. Looks like hard work? Not necessarily. The effect can be achieved with self-seeding perennials and annuals, which mostly look after themselves, and generally tend to include old-fashioned flowers such as foxgloves (*digitalis purpurea*), aquilegia, marigolds (*calendula*) forget-me-nots (*myosotis*), phlox, and sweet williams (*dianthus barbatus*).

Pink aquilegia, self-seeded

The original cottage gardens also had to provide food for the householder, and would have included herbs and vegetables – so if you don't fancy having a formal vegetable bed in the garden then why not grow garlic, spinach or runner beans amongst your flowers?

Herbaceous borders

These borders are the ones you can see at stately homes – very grand and meticulously planned. This is a more formal planting, so requires more work in the form of staking tall plants and weeding out any self-seeded plants. This border generally consists of summer and early-autumn flowering plants and once the season has ended, there's not much to look at. In the average-sized garden, it is best to opt for a mixed border.

Tip

If you need to stake tall plants, cut old tights or stockings into strips and use to tie plants to the stakes instead of twine, which can sometimes cut into the stem.

Mixed borders

As the name suggests, this includes a bit of everything, and means that you can have something to look at all year round. You can include shrubs to add height and structure, and if evergreen, will keep interest in the winter; spring bulbs such as daffodils, crocus and tulips, which will appear before the summer flowers get into full swing; and then you can add annuals to fill in any gaps.

Gravel gardens

Most often associated with Japanese gardens, gravel gardens are ideally suited for anyone with a minimum amount of time to spend in the garden, as once established, they are easy to look after. And in areas where drought is becoming more common, it makes sense, instead of lawns and borders, to have that space made up of surfaces such as gravel, decking or cobbles. Interest and decoration are then provided with ornaments and architectural plants such as New Zealand flax (*phormium*) or bamboo, and plants in large eye-catching pots.

'Contemporary gravel garden'
Best in Show, Chelsea Flower Show, 2010

Prairie planting

This is a style of planting that has become very fashionable over the last few years. The more traditional lawns and borders have been replaced with low-maintenance perennials and ornamental grasses, planted in swathes, with a gravel or stone path winding through. Again, this is ideal for those whose time spent in the garden is limited, and an advantage is that it certainly doesn't need to look neat and tidy.

First steps in planting

Buying plants

This is, for me, one of the most exciting and pleasurable aspects of gardening, but a word of warning here – buying plants can become addictive. I have lost count of the number of times I have bought too many plants, got them home, and then wondered 'where on earth am I going to put them?' If you can be disciplined, you will manage much better than I used to.

Eventually I learned that before you go to the garden centre or nursery, you have to make a list. It may seem obvious, but it is so easy, once you see all those lovely plants, to forget just what it was you had planned.

But if you do impulse buy, make sure that you have checked the conditions the plant needs and that it will grow in your garden – see soil type (in Chapter 1) and hardiness (Chapter 3).

Also be aware of just how large in height and spread a particular plant will grow and that you have the space for it – if you get this wrong, you could end up with an expensive mistake. But don't feel too bad; every gardener does it at some point.

Plant nursery

And these days you really don't need to go far to buy plants – even supermarkets sell them. But do take the time to check the plants over carefully wherever you buy them. If you are still rather unsure about what you require, I would recommend that you go to a reputable nursery, who grow their own stock, and who would advise you if a plant is suitable for the conditions in your garden. If you feel more confident, then you can go to one of the big busy garden centres, which has a fast turnover of stock, and the likelihood is that the plants are fresh and healthy.

Which brings me to the points to look out for when you are buying plants:

- Check that the plant actually matches the label – these can accidentally get mixed up;
- Make sure that the pots have all been well watered, as plants that are too dry will be stressed;
- Make sure that the leaves are healthy looking without blemishes;
- Avoid plants that are damaged, lopsided or have broken stems;
- If the surface of the compost has weeds, pull them out – you don't want to take weeds home with you;
- Roots coming through the base of the pot are fine indicating that the plant has established a healthy root system. And if necessary the pot can be cut away carefully to remove the plant.

It may seem obvious to say this, but do take care when transporting the plants home and avoid damage to stems and leaves, keeping the pot upright if you can. And when you get your new plants home, aim to plant them out, whether in your borders or in containers, as soon as possible, certainly within a few days.

Planting out in the garden

To help the plant get the best start in its new home, soak the pot in water until the compost is thoroughly moist immediately before you plant it out – this will make it easier for the roots to establish.

Here are just a few points to remember:

- Make sure the soil is prepared (see Chapter 1) and weed free;
- If you are planting a shrub or tree that will become a permanent feature of your garden, dig a hole at least one-and-a-half times the size of the pot, sprinkle some general fertiliser into the hole and fork in (follow instructions on the pack for quantity), make sure the soil is not compacted;
- Check which way the plant looks best – put it in the hole and stand back and take a look, and make sure that the plant is upright and not leaning;
- Keep the root ball level with the surface of the soil;
- Fill in the soil around the root ball (this is called back filling) and firm in gently to ensure there are no air pockets;

- Water in well, thoroughly soaking the soil. If you are planting a tree or shrub, you can make a small moat around the plant and keep filling that with water; this directs the water to the roots and helps prevent the water flowing away from the plant.

If you have stuck to your shopping list, you will of course know where each of your plants is going to be situated. If however, you have made an impulse purchase – or several – take the time to read the label to find out just what conditions the plant likes, whether in full sun or shade, and also how big it will grow. This will help you to find the right site for the plant.

Tip

If you are at all unsure that you will remember the names of your new plants after planting out, then either put the pot label in beside your plant, or if you don't like the look of that, keep the label safely – it will also give any pruning advice if needed.

Planting in containers

As with planting in the garden, make sure that the plant has had a good soaking before you transfer it to its new container, and then just follow these simple steps:

- To give adequate drainage, cover the hole(s) in the base of the pot with broken crocks, or broken up polystyrene (which makes the pot less heavy);

- Make sure you put any large containers into their final position before filling with compost and plants, as they can become too heavy to move safely;

- If you want to use water-retaining gel or fertiliser pellets at this stage, then follow the instructions on the pack ;

- Fill the pot about half way with multi-purpose compost;

- Arrange your plants in the pot – remember how big the plant will grow, so don't cram too many into too small a pot;

- Top up the pot with compost, with the root ball level with the surface of the compost, but leave space at the top so that when you water it doesn't flow straight over the sides;

- Gently firm the compost around the plants;

- Water the pot well;

- Place the pot on pot feet to help with drainage.

Planting in hanging baskets

There are a couple of different types of hanging baskets. Those, as in the illustration below made from rattan, which look very attractive, are planted in a similar way to a container. But just make sure that the plastic lining is punctured to aid drainage.

The other main type is the wire basket, which gives you the opportunity to plant in the sides as well as the top of the basket. Here's how to do it:

Begonias in a hanging basket

- Place your basket on a pot or bucket to keep it stable and move the chains out of the way;
- Line the basket with coconut fibre, or most garden centres now sell purpose-made basket liners, then add a piece of punctured plastic liner to reduce water loss, making sure it is not visible;

- Start to fill the basket with compost, mixed with fertiliser and water-retaining gel, if you are using;

- Once you have about two inches of compost in the basket, make three cuts in the plastic and liner about one inch across, evenly spaced around the basket.

- Select three plants, protect the root ball by wrapping in paper or card; push each plant through from the outside of the basket, until the root ball is snug against the liner, remove the paper and firm the soil round the rootballs;

- Continue to fill the basket with compost to about two thirds of the way up, and make three more cuts in the plastic and liner;

- Place three more plants as with the previous layer;

- Fill up with compost to within about one inch of the top of the basket;

- Now you can place the remainder of your plants on the top, and firm the soil around them;

- Water well and hang outside once all danger of frost is past.

Planting bulbs

There is a very simple rule to follow when you're planting bulbs and that is to **plant the bulb three times its own depth**, which is quite a bit deeper than most people think it should be. So a daffodil bulb, for example,

34

would need to be planted into a hole about 7 inches (18–19 cms) deep, assuming the bulb is around 2 inches in depth.

This means that the chances of digging up or damaging bulbs when you are weeding or planting out summer bedding are drastically reduced. But note that crocus bulbs, because they are so much smaller will, of course, be closer to the surface.

Snowdrops are treated slightly differently, in that the bulbs are purchased 'in the green', that is, after flowering and before the leaves have died back.

Tip

For spring-flowering bulbs, plant crocus before the end of September, daffodils before the end of October, and tulips from October to the end of November.

If you have a number of bulbs to plant, you can get a special bulb planter, which not only makes the job a little quicker, but it has markings on the side to give you the depth.

Caring for your plants

Having chosen your plants, taken them home and planted them out, is that it, and all you have to do now is admire them? Well, no. All plants need a certain amount of after-care, and one of the most obvious and important is...

Watering

When plants are establishing themselves in the first few months, and transplanting them can cause some stress, they really do need to be watered regularly – even those planted out in the borders, and even if it rains. Get into the habit of watering new plants every week – not just a sprinkle, give them a good soak.

Plants in containers need to be kept an eye on, and watered every day – don't wait for the plants to wilt before watering, you may have left it too late.

Once you have thoroughly watered your borders and your new plants, you can cover the soil with a layer of mulch – usually home-made compost – that helps to conserve the moisture in the soil and prevent it drying out too quickly.

In many areas now, water conservation has become an important issue, so it is a very good idea to invest in a water butt. These are widely available, not expensive, and easy to connect to a down pipe – and also a lot easier than 'to-ing' and 'fro-ing' from the kitchen tap with a watering can.

The best time to water in hot weather is in the evening, as the water tends to evaporate during the day, and in cold and dull weather it is best to water in the morning. In extremely hot weather, aim to water twice a day. But watering at any time is better than not watering at all – even at midday if your pot plants are starting to wilt, just be careful to avoid wetting the leaves too much as the water could cause them to scorch in the hot sun.

During hot, dry weather don't worry about watering grass even if it's looking brown, it will green up again as soon as it rains. Similarly with established shrubs and trees – their roots go down a long way to reach moisture, and watering will have little effect except possibly to encourage those roots to come back up to the surface which could de-stabilise a tree or large shrub.

Tip

To make it easier to water hanging baskets, cut off the top of a plastic drinks bottle, about 4–5 inches, and push this upside down into the centre of the basket – you can pour water from your watering can or hosepipe directly into the bottle, which acts as a funnel to direct water straight to the plant roots, instead of water running out over the sides of the basket.

Feeding

To get the best out of your plants, they do need feeding, and although they will still grow and flower if you only water them, if you also feed them the difference can be amazing.

Containers

For plants in containers and hanging baskets, a liquid feed (fertiliser) is beneficial from spring to summer, when the plants are growing and flowering – they will grow bigger, have more flowers and generally be a lot stronger and healthier. Little and often is best, but aim to feed every two weeks at least. Read the instructions on the pack for the right dose and water in using a watering can.

Slow-release feed in the form of pellets or sticks are an alternative if you are likely to forget to feed and you normally water your plants using a hose. Again, check the instructions on the pack as to the quantity required and how often they should be replaced, as they may not last all season.

Beds and borders

Fertiliser sold in powder or granular form is cheap and easy to use. There are different concentrations of the three main elements, nitrogen (N), phosphorus (P) and potassium (K) for different uses, so you can buy a fertiliser specifically for roses, or fruit trees, for example.

You will easily find one for general-purpose use – sprinkle thinly around the plant, ideally when the soil is damp and gently fork it in. The best time to do this is in spring, just as the plants are starting to put on new growth. These fertilisers are long lasting, so once you have done this at the start of the season, you won't need to do it again until the following year.

Foliar feeding

In some circumstances, you can foliar feed your border plants (that's feeding through the leaves) with a liquid feed. This can be used as an emergency treatment if a plant is looking a bit forlorn, or is reluctant to grow and seems in need of a boost, as this type of feed takes effect much more quickly.

Weeding

I may be stating the obvious here, but if you can do some weeding little and often, it can make your life much easier. Yes, I know that weeding is a job that everyone thinks they hate doing and that it's a real bore, but if you have a garden of any size, then you will have weeds – they can even turn up in containers.

Try not to turn this into too much of a chore – instead just make a point of pulling out a few weeds as you walk round the garden each day.

Of course what is difficult for most new gardeners is to tell the difference between weeds and plants that have self-seeded – in my garden each year I acquire new plants for free this way, especially aquilegia (as in the picture above), forget-me-not (*myosotis*) and foxgloves (*digitalis*). Telling the difference will come with experience, but the best way I found initially was to let the seedling grow and see what it turns into. If you think it is a weed, then make sure you pull or dig it out before it flowers and sets seed.

Unless you want a show garden, a few weeds here and there are no big deal – so don't become obsessive about it and a few green weeds look better than bare soil. But do keep an eye on them, as they are great survivors and will take over your borders and strangle your plants if left to get out of hand.

However, perennial weeds that come up every year such as brambles, nettles and dandelions are a real nuisance, and it is worth spending time to get every piece of root out that you can, as these plants will grow again from even the tiniest section left in the ground. And don't be tempted to put these on the compost heap – you will find that they take that over as well. (More about weeds in Chapter 4.)

Pruning

How, where and when do I prune? This is a question guaranteed to send most novice gardeners running for cover, and there are certainly whole books devoted to this subject alone. However, I'm going to keep this simple, as there are just a few things that a new gardener needs to be aware of.

First, there are three basic pruning tools a beginner gardener needs:

- Secateurs – can vary in price, so buy the one you feel you can afford and that feels comfortable in your hands;
- Loppers – secateurs on long arms, the longer the arms and the heavier the loppers, the more effective they are. Some have extendable arms. But try them out before buying as, if they are too heavy, you won't use them!
- Pruning saw – invaluable in cutting small branches or stems too large for secateurs, and some come with a fold-away blade for safety.

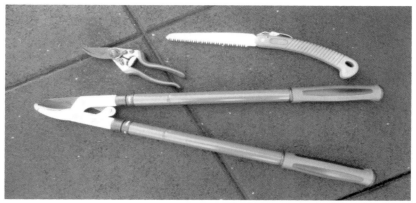

Loppers, secateurs and pruning saw

One simple method of pruning is dead-heading. And this is exactly what is says, taking dead flower

41

heads off the plant. If you are tidy-minded, this keeps the plant looking trim, but it also encourages the plant to produce new flowers to prolong the flowering period, especially useful for summer hanging baskets and containers. Different types of plant require a slightly different technique:

- Bulbs: pinch off the flowers only and leave the stalk, as the nutrients in the stalk and the leaves are needed by the bulb to help it flower in the following year;

- Roses: a single flower can be pinched off between thumb and first finger. If a whole cluster has faded, then cut back with secateurs, about 6 inches (15 cms) to just above a leaf joint, or just above a new shoot, if you see one;

- A single head of flowers on a long stalk, as in pelargoniums: take off the whole flower head and stalk, pinching it out where the stalk joins the main stem;

- Short-stalked flowers, such as fuchsias: just snap off individual flowers;

- Lavender (see the picture below) and heather: once the flowers start to fade, it is best to cut the stalks back with shears – but be careful not to cut back into the old growth. This method can also be used with marjoram (oregano).

Apart from the human need to be neat and tidy, and to keep our plants a manageable size, there are good reasons for pruning:

- to cut out dead or diseased wood from trees and shrubs;
- to cut back branches that have become crossed over to prevent damage;
- and to promote new and strong growth.

Otherwise, pruning is not always necessary and depends on the type of plants you have in your garden. For most shrubs, use your common sense – if it becomes unruly or lopsided, or if there are dead or damaged stems, then cut those stems out.

The most likely candidates for regular pruning are roses, fruit trees, clematis and spring-flowering shrubs, such as forsythia, as well as shrubs grown for their winter stem colour such as dogwoods (*cornus*).

So how exactly do you prune? Here are some simple rules:

- Where to cut – always cut just above a leaf joint or bud (this is called a node) and angle the cut away from the new bud.

- If a shrub flowers in spring or early summer, prune immediately after flowering – cut out the oldest and thickest of the stems at ground level, taking out about one third of all stems. The most well known plants in this group are forsythia, flowering currant (*ribes*) and mock orange (*philadelphus*). The reason for this is that the flowers are produced on the previous year's growth, so after pruning the plant will grow during the summer and it is these new stems that produce flowers the following spring.

- If the shrub flowers in the summer leave pruning until early spring – it's best to wait until the worst of the frost is past – as the flowers appear on the same year's new growth. This applies to spirea, buddleia, abelia and Himalayan honeysuckle (*leycestaria*). These plants can be cut right back if you are tight for space and want to control the plant's size.

- Dogwoods (*cornus*) can be cut right back to the ground in early spring as it is the new year's growth that gives the vibrant colour to the stems during the winter.

- Clematis – some need pruning a little, some need to be cut back hard, and some don't need pruning at all. As I don't want to turn this into a book about how to prune clematis, my best advice is, if you are buying a clematis, keep the label, which will give pruning advice. If you inherit one, and don't know which group it falls into, take one of the flowers into your local nursery who be able to identify if and give you the right advice on whether or when to prune.

- Roses – as with clematis, there are different groups of roses requiring slightly different types of pruning. Again, check the label or talk to your local nursery. Apart from pruning, however, roses do need to be dead-headed regularly to encourage further flowering.

Whatever you are planning to cut back, make sure that your secateurs or loppers are sharp and clean. If the blades are blunted at all, then there is a chance that you can snag the stem or branch, which could lead to more permanent damage. And working with equipment that has not been cleaned after the previous use, could lead to transmission of disease from one plant to another.

Climbing rose, 'Paul Scarlet'

Chapter 3

The Gardening Year

Climate zones

I wanted to mention something about climate zones, as I am aware that many readers of this book will live in vastly different areas from, perhaps, a hot, dry environment through to near-arctic conditions. In these circumstances, it is difficult to be precise about what plants to grow. The US Department of Agriculture divided the USA into 11 different climate zones – zone 1 being the coldest, to zone 11 the hottest – which give an indication of how cold it gets in winter. And in the UK we have also adopted this classification, so that most nurseries, plant encyclopaedias and plant catalogues now provide this information.

Once you know which zone you live in, it is much easier to find out which plants will survive your winter and which won't.

Here in the UK, most of the country falls into zone 8, around the west coasts is zone 9, there is a small part of the Scottish highlands, which is much colder at zone 7, and the very tip of west Cornwall ,which falls into zone 10, is very mild – although occasionally we do have exceptionally cold winter weather.

Snow in Cornwall

Keep in mind also, that there are other factors that can affect the survival of plants in winter – altitude and whether your garden is north or south facing. If you are unsure, check out your neighbours' gardens, see what they are growing, talk to them, and also talk to your local nursery.

So what does this mean in practice?

Remember that the lower the number, the colder the winter. So if you live in zone 8 and you want to grow a plant that is hardy to zone 9, then you will need either to keep it in a pot and bring it indoors or under cover during the winter, or keep if protected with horticultural fleece – or as a cheaper alternative, bubble wrap works well as insulation.

A quick word about weather: it's not just frost that can damage your plants. Also watch out for torrential rain, gales, and scorching sun. Inevitably, there will be occasions when the plants in your garden suffer damage but, most of the time though, they will recover. Gardeners often end up becoming 'weather watchers' and each evening catch up with their local forecast on the radio or TV – I certainly do now, and woe betide anyone who rings me while I'm watching the weather forecast.

Gardening all year round

To get the most pleasure from a garden, the aim is to have as much happening as possible, for as much of the year as possible. And this is one of the most fascinating aspects of gardening – the constant change; nothing ever stays the same.

When I first started gardening, I very much wanted to get the garden looking 'just right' and for it to remain looking 'just right'. I soon realised that nature doesn't work that way. Gardening is rather like a journey – you visit villages and landscapes and think how lovely they are, but you take photos and move on to see new villages and landscapes. And that's how it is with a garden – a leisurely journey – always moving on.

However, back now to practicalities, even if all you have is a container garden in the back yard, you can still have interest all year round. So I'm going to give just a few suggestions as to what plants are at their best during the different parts of the year. This is certainly not an exhaustive list, but it will give you a starting point.

Spring

For most people, spring bulbs, and especially daffodils, herald the arrival of spring in the garden, and having clumps in your borders or in containers is certainly cheering after the winter. It's better, if your space is limited, to choose dwarf daffodils, as once the flowers are gone, the leaves that will die down naturally are less obvious and untidy as those of the larger more showy daffodils.

Azalea, variety unknown

You can start off in early spring with crocus and move on through daffodils to tulips and hyacinths – again great in containers. I usually move my bulb containers into a position by the front door as the new shoots appear, then after flowering, I give the plants a feed and put the pots at the back of the garden, out of the way for the rest of the year.

Pansies and violas can provide instant colour in the garden, and are readily available from nurseries at this time of year.

Shrubs can also give you colour later in spring. You don't need a great deal of space and some, like camellias and rhododendrons or azaleas, which need an acid soil, look great in containers (just make sure you use ericaceous compost). Both of these are evergreen so provide interest all year. Other spring flowering shrubs include forsythia, flowering currant (*ribes*) and viburnum amongst the more well known.

Summer

I wondered where to start with summer flowers, because you really are spoiled for choice. Summer bedding immediately springs to mind with the colourful displays seen every summer in public parks and gardens. Nurseries and garden centres have masses of trays of plants ready to be planted straight into your borders, containers and hanging baskets, and whatever colour takes your fancy you will be probably be able to find it – so this becomes a personal choice as to which plants you choose.

Nasturtiums and surfinia summer bedding

Among the most popular are pelargoniums (often called geraniums, although not to be confused with hardy geraniums), petunias, tobacco plant (*nicotiana*), busy lizzies (*impatiens*), cone flower (*rudbeckia*) and verbenas. Other popular plants, which are easy to grow from seed, as the seeds are quite large, are sweet peas (*lathyrus odora-*

tus), marigolds (*calendula*) and nasturtiums (*tropaeolum majus*). All of these plants, when they finish flowering, are generally taken up and thrown away at the end of the season (on the compost heap if you have one).

On a more permanent basis, herbaceous perennials are the heart of a garden in summer – lupins, hardy geraniums, delphiniums, red hot pokers (*kniphofia*), irises and penstemons – it's a very long list, so pick what you like and check that it will grow in the conditions in your garden. Foliage plants, such as hostas and grasses can provide a wonderful setting for the flowers.

Roses are the most popular flowers in British gardens. Now I know that for new gardeners, roses appear rather like the prima donnas of the garden – prickly and difficult to care for with just a brief glorious show of flowers, because that's exactly how I felt. I inherited a couple of roses when I moved to my present house but I've discovered that, in fact, they are not as bad as I thought, and I have since bought a couple more.

There are now new versions of the old-fashioned roses, which means you are able to get compact patio roses for containers and carpet roses for ground cover with repeat flowering. These newer roses are lower maintenance, just requiring deadheading to encourage new flowers, and a trim back at the end of the season.

White carpet rose

Autumn

The foliage of trees and shrubs provides the main colours of autumn, and you certainly don't need a large garden to enjoy them.

Deciduous azaleas as well as some of the Japanese maples (*acer palmatum*) can provide spectacular red or yellow foliage colours in autumn. Berries and fruits can also provide colour – cotoneasters and pyracanthas are two that spring to mind – as well as supplying valuable food for birds.

55

And there are still flowers that can give a show of colour at this time of year, though many of the summer perennials will continue to flower into autumn. Among specific autumn-flowering plants are:

- Japanese anemones, tall and stately flowers, mostly shades of pink, but there is also one with beautiful white flowers;
- Heleniums with daisy-like flowers in warm yellows and oranges (the common name for helenium is 'sneezeweed' because apparently early American settlers used it to make snuff);
- A very reliable plant is *sedum spectabile* (ice plant), loved by butterflies and it flowers for ages;

Schizostylis coccinea major

- One of my favourites is the kaffir lily (*schizostylis coccinea*) shown in the picture above, with pretty red or pink flowers, and also a delicate white, that requires very little maintenance – for the best effect you need to have a big clump of them, but they do spread each year if you can only afford a couple of plants to start.

Winter

Hellebore, flowering in winter

Yes, there are flowers for winter, though admittedly not a great number. Amongst the most beautiful are the hellebore family, including the hellebore or Christmas rose

57

(*helleborus niger*) with white flowers and *helleborus orientalis* that have green or pink or purple flowers. These plants are trouble free and self-seed easily giving you new plants for free.

Other possibilities are winter-flowering pansies – what a versatile plant this is – and ornamental cabbages (*brassica oleracea*), in striking colours of red, pink or cream. They have been used extensively by public parks departments in the last few years, so they may not be to your taste. And of course, snowdrops, that make their appearance during January.

Evergreen plants provide continuing interest in the garden during winter, and conifers come into their own at this time of year. They don't have to be large and fast growing – you can get dwarf, slow-growing conifers. One of my favourites is juniper, and though also available in green, grey or yellow, the one I have, *juniperus squamata* 'Blue Carpet' is a beautiful steel blue-grey colour. Combine these with the coloured stems of dogwoods, *cornus alba* for red stems and *cornus stolonifera* for yellow, and you really can have a colourful garden.

Another way to keep interest in the winter garden is to leave the seed heads on perennial plants such as grasses; leave the skeletons of bronze fennel (*foeniculum 'purpureum'*) or the old flower heads of sedum spectabile – they can look really beautiful on a frosty morning. So don't be too quick to cut down these dead-looking stems, as they also help to protect the crown of the plant during cold weather.

It is possible, with just a little planning, to have colour and interest in the garden all year, and any blank spots can always be brightened up with containers filled with whatever flowers are looking good at that time of year.

Zebra grass (*miscanthus zebrinus)*

Chapter 4

Friends and Enemies in the Garden

I want to start with the gardener's enemies, and get the bad news out of the way first, before moving on to the good news.

Weeds

You've got your garden planned and planted, and you're feeling pleased you've got this far. So I now want to cover some aspects of gardening that can prove difficult for a new gardener. And one of these is the subject of weeds.

There's an old saying, 'a weed is any plant growing in the wrong place'. But this is true only up to a point, as there are plants that are always weeds wherever they grow. And weeds are not always the same as wild flowers, many of which are now grown deliberately in wildflower gardens (for those with the space) and plants such as foxgloves (*digitalis purpurea*) are very welcome in a garden border where they will happily self-seed.

There are two main types of weed.

Annual weeds

As the name suggests, these weeds grow each year, flower, produce seed and die. Well, that's fine you might think but unfortunately, the seeds they spread can quickly take over your borders and your whole garden.

Tip

The best time to pull out weeds is after rain – the ground is soft and they will come out, complete with roots, a lot easier than when the soil is dry and baked hard.

Most gardening books will tell you to remove them before they flower to prevent the spread of seeds, but this can be difficult if you don't know what weed seedlings look like. What I had to do was wait until the flowers appeared so that I could identify whether they were weeds or not. You have to be quick at this point – if you leave it too long, the plant will have set seed and hey presto, they will be all over the garden before you know it. Weed flowers are generally small and insignificant, but a good gardening book will have pictures to help with identification.

Annual weeds are easily pulled up and can be put straight on to your compost heap, if you have one, but again, only before they set seed.

Here are some examples of annual weeds (and I've given the Latin names as I'm aware that the common names may not be known everywhere):

- chickweed (*stellania media*),
- groundsel (*senecio vulgaris*),
- hairy bitter cress (*cardamine hirsute*),
- goosegrass (*galium aparine*), and
- daisy (*bellis perennis*).

Other annual weeds such as the opium poppy (*papaver somniferum*) and Welsh poppy (*mecanopsis cambrica*) are really very pretty and can be left in the garden if they are in the right place, and you can always take out the seedlings if there are too many.

Which weeds turn up in your garden does depend on the climate and type of soil you have, but they can be dealt with fairly easily. Unlike …

Perennial weeds

Now these really are 'thugs' in any garden, and if you have taken over an untended or neglected garden, you will have many of these to deal with before you even start (see the section on preparing the ground in Chapter 1).

These plants have remarkable self-preservation and if they weren't such a nuisance, you could almost admire them – I did say almost!

Some have very long, deep roots (called tap roots) which makes it extremely difficult, once the plant is established, to pull them out in one go, for example, dandelions. Others have underground runners, which can spread the plant quite some distance very quickly, as in buttercups. In either case, if you're not able to get every piece of root out of the ground, they just re-grow.

Tip

If you keep cutting back these perennial weeds, either with a hoe or shears, you will dramatically weaken the plants' roots and they will eventually die, though this can take a while.

Now don't despair —you will probably only have one or two of these monsters to deal with. Among the most familiar are:

- Greater bindweed (*calystegia silvatica*) – fast growing climber with large white trumpet shaped flowers, which climbs round garden plants and eventually smothers them;

- Ground elder (*aegopodium podagravia*) – spreads via underground roots to form a thick ground cover;

- Creeping buttercup (*ranunculus repens*) – has underground runners making it difficult to get all the roots out: it's important to remember that this plant is also poisonous to guinea pigs (cavies);

64

- Ragwort (*senecio jacobaea*) – although this plant is a food source for some insects, it is extremely poisonous to livestock, so it is better removed and destroyed, as even the dead plant can be lethal;

- Tree seedlings – if you have trees nearby, keep an eye out for seedlings and pull them out while they are still small – once the roots are established, they'll be much harder to shift;

- Japanese knotweed – this is a real tough customer and I have seen some amazing film of this particular plant pushing its way through concrete. There have been trials in the UK of a biological control which may well be available to gardeners within around 5–10 years.

I take a fairly laid back approach to weeds in general, but do try and keep them in their place.

I have dandelions (*taraxacum officinale*), but don't worry about them at all as I have two guinea pigs that love them, so they are picked regularly – yes they regrow, but then they are picked again. This illustration shows the flower heads and the familiar seed head as well as part of the long tap root.

Another perennial weed I have is the stinging nettle (*urtica dioica*). I don't like this plant as I have a bad reaction to the 'sting', but I do leave a patch in the corner of the garden, as it is a magnet for wildlife.

I also have brambles (*rubus fruticosus*). Again, I try and keep them in one corner of the garden as, although it takes a lot of work to keep them from spreading, I do enjoy the blackberries they provide each autumn – especially in blackberry and apple pie.

Wild ivy (*hedera helix*) is another plant I happily live with, as it is a great habitat for wildlife. Although it won't harm trees or shrubs, it can damage walls, so just be aware of that.

So how do you get rid of these persistent weeds? Don't be tempted to rotavate the ground, as this will simply chop up the roots and encourage even more growth. If you have a large patch to deal with, use a glyphosate-based weed killer, which is safe for pets and wildlife once it is dry, and the ground is ready for planting once you have cleared the ground. The best time to do this is in spring, when most plants are growing strongly.

Tip

Apply a teaspoon of salt carefully to individual weeds and they will die.

Alternatively, you can chop the plants down to the ground, and if you don't want to dig the roots out, then a flame gun is very useful to kill the new shoots as they appear (do make sure to take care in the vicinity of other plants, and follow the safety instructions). This won't be instant death for these weeds, and you may need to do this several times, but if you combine this with digging the roots out then you will get rid of them much sooner.

If these weeds appear between established plants in your borders, then the only option is to hand weed and get as much of the roots out as you can.

Prevention

To prevent weeds in the first place sounds like a good idea? Well yes, but this is easier said than done, as no garden is ever going to be completely weed-free. However there are a couple of options that might help:

Mulching

This is not completely guaranteed to prevent weeds. It won't kill existing perennial weeds as they can grow through the mulch. But as it also improves the soil, mulching is worth doing anyway. The best time to do this is in the spring – make sure the beds and borders are as weed-free as you can make them and the soil is moist, as this helps to prevent moisture loss.

There are different types of mulch you can use:

- For beds and borders, garden compost, if you have it, provides a rich source of nutrients, but has to be replaced every year. It could well be worth buying some from your local garden centre.

- Or if you have a border with mainly shrubs, which won't be touched for a while, a mulch of bark chippings can look good, and this can last for two or three years.

- Gravel makes an attractive mulch, which will obviously last for a long while, though it won't add nutrients to the soil. It is ideal for a rock garden where it can help prevent smaller plants becoming damaged by rain and mud splashes.

- A new mulch, recently on the market, is cocoa shell. It is lightweight, smells of chocolate, but can be more expensive. This would need renewing every year. **Warning**: this is not suitable if you have dogs, as it is highly toxic to them.

Tip

For plants that thrive in acidic conditions, such as camellias, heathers and blueberries, use coffee grounds as a mulch around the plant.

Weed-proof membrane

A membrane can be used beneath a mulch of bark or gravel. It is permanent and its use is therefore limited, as it is not then possible to put more plants in that border, but certainly could be useful for, say, a gravel pathway.

It is hard work to install and can look really ugly if it shows through, so think carefully before you try this.

Now I don't want to put a further damper on things at this stage, but I do need to mention a few of the gardeners' enemies in the form of mobile ones!

Slugs and snails

Of all the pests that can cause problems for gardeners, probably the most talked about and hated are slugs and snails. The damage they can do to plants is spectacular and heartbreaking, especially if you live in a damp climate, as they just love moist and humid conditions.

Slug damage to a seedling

Both can be identified by the slime trails they leave behind, leaving holes in leaves and even eating the whole plant, but there are slight differences between the two. Slugs live in the soil and generally only attack the lower part of the plant, whereas snails are excellent climbers and can quite easily find their way into hanging baskets and even on to balconies. Both are active mostly at night.

Tip

If you have a real slug and snail problem, it is not a good idea to water your plants in the evening as this creates the ideal damp conditions that they love as they come out to feed.

Prevention

There are chemicals, such as slug pellets, that will effectively kill slugs and snails and protect your plants. But bear in mind that although birds and small mammals, such as frogs and hedgehogs, probably won't eat the brightly coloured pellets, they may well be poisoned by eating the dead slugs and snails, which will be highly toxic. And be especially aware in spring, when blackbirds and thrushes may feed these to their babies.

But there are alternatives:

- Biological controls are available for killing slugs. These are available by mail order only, so check out organic gardening supplies' websites for more information.

- You can use barriers around plants, such as crushed eggshells, grit, bran, or wood-ash or soot (if you have a multi-fuel stove or know a chimney sweep). You will have varying degrees of success, so give them a try and see which works best.

- Smear petroleum jelly thickly around the rims of pots, or you can purchase copper tape, which you can stick around the pot sides – this give the snail a small electric shock. These will be more effective against snails than slugs.

- One of the best deterrents, for both slugs and snails, is the use of beer traps. You can buy these from a garden centre – or improvise by cutting off the base of plastic water or coke bottles, about three inches deep. Place the trap, filled with cheap beer, in a hole with the top just above soil level. This is the method that appeals to me the most, as they crawl in and drown – but at least they die happy. You can also use out of date fruit juice, or even milk just about on the turn. It's surprising just how many you can catch this way. But do remember to change the traps every couple of days, otherwise it all starts to ferment – which is not at all pleasant.

- Another excellent way to get rid of these pests is to collect them up in the late evening, when they start to become active and – if you're not too squeamish – drown them in a bucket of heavily salted wa-water. Plain water will not work. I once spent half an hour collecting slugs and snails happily throwing them into a bucket of water, thinking they would drown, but a short time later, they were swarming up the side of the bucket and away. It's the salt that kills them, and if you are very hard hearted you can sprinkle salt directly on to the slug or snail, but salt will also damage your plants, so do this carefully.

- You can go on a snail and slug hunt during the day as well, as they tend to spend daylights hours hiding in dark, damp corners, under foliage and under stones.

- Check the base of your pots first thing in the morning, especially if you have seedlings or young plants, and you will probably find a couple of slugs tucked into the drainage holes, resting after a night's feasting – they're usually small, so just squish them.

- A very successful method of protecting special plants or seedlings in pots is to stand the pot on a support or pot feet, placed in a shallow container or large saucer of water. This water acts as a moat and I have yet to find any snail willing to make that crossing.

To lessen the heartache of losing your prized plants to these slimy monsters, why not grow plants that the slugs and snails actually don't like? I've listed those that I have so far discovered and now grow them in my own garden:

- Shrubs such as forsythia, fuschia, azalea, camellia, pieris, buddleia, spirea, hebe, honeysuckle (*lonicera*), jasmine, and pheasant berry (*leycestaria*);
- Just about all grasses;
- Herbs, for instance, rosemary, oregano, fennel, bay, lavender and sage, though be careful with chives and parsley as the slugs do seem to like them;
- Hardy perennials such as hardy geraniums, penstemon, crocosmia, heathers, Japanese anemone, roses, osteospermums, hellebores, kaffir lilies (*schizostylis*), euphorbia, evening primrose (*oenothera*), ajuga, achillea, musk mallow (*malva*) and *dierama* (angels' fishing rods);
- In addition, biennials, such as foxgloves and forget-me-nots (*myositis*).

I am discovering more plants each year, but it's an ongoing quest to outwit these voracious creatures.

73

Other garden pests

Caterpillars

They make holes in leaves in much the same way as snails, but without the slime trail, and they are easily visible during the day. The worst offenders are those of the cabbage white butterfly, who lay clutches of eggs on the underside of leaves, particularly nasturtium – and, of course, plants in the cabbage  family (seen here) – so there can then be dozens of caterpillars who will munch their way through the leaves doing a great deal of damage. They can even destroy whole plants very quickly.

If you see this white butterfly in your garden, do a quick check under the leaves, pick off any leaves with eggs or caterpillars and either squish, or put them on the bird table. Solitary caterpillars can be left alone, as they really don't cause that much damage.

Aphids

Aphids come in different colours, brown, white, black and green. Although I believe it's the green ones that are true aphids, the others do behave in the same way though – they suck the sap of fresh new plant growth.

But before you reach for the insecticidal spray, which will also kill the beneficial insects, you can get rid of them in other ways.

The easiest is just to brush them off the plant with your fingers – if you are squeamish, or there are too many, wear disposable gloves – but do be careful not to damage the plant's growing tip.

I also discovered that ants will 'milk' the aphids for a sweet sugary substance they excrete that the ants love. In return, the ants protect the aphids from their natural predators. But here is a great tip: put jam or honey on to the plant below the aphids. The ants will lap that up and will no longer need the aphids. Within a few days, the aphids' predators, such as birds, or ladybird larvae can get on with their job of feeding on the aphids.

Tip

Plant a clove of garlic by the base of a rose bush (plant mid-winter) and the rose will be free of greenfly – the garlic acts as systemic insecticide and the rose absorbs this through its root system. Alternatively, crush and boil some garlic bulbs, add a teaspoon of washing up liquid, and use the liquid as a spray to control aphids.

Encourage birds into your garden, as they just love insects, aphids and caterpillars. One day, not long after I moved to Cornwall, I noticed some aphids on the stem of one of my roses, but by the time I had put my gloves on (yes, I'm squeamish), I noticed that a sparrow was working his way up and down the stem of the rose, picking at it, so I waited, not wanting to disturb the bird. When I went back to the rose a while later, the aphids were all gone.

Now I hardly ever have aphids on my plants and I watch the sparrows and blue-tits checking out my plants regularly.

Vine weevil

Vine weevil mostly attack pot plants. The adults, small, slow-moving, brown beetles, fortunately can't fly; however, they can climb. I recently found one inside the house on the wall of the first floor landing and I have no idea how it got there. Needless to say, it didn't get any further. They nibble the leaves of plants, leaving horseshoe shapes around the edges.

But it's the larvae, small white c-shaped grubs, in the soil that cause the most damage by eating the roots of the plants, and the first you will probably know about it is when the plant dies. This picture will help you identify the adult weevil.

Protect your pots by covering the compost with a layer of grit, which will help prevent the weevil laying its eggs in the pot soil. There is an organic biological control, as well as a chemical pesticide, that you can water on to prevent attack during spring to autumn.

Ants

No garden will ever be entirely free of ants, whether they're black, red or yellow. If the nest is likely to cause a nuisance, say by the house or on the patio, then you can destroy the nests by pouring on boiling water – though they will probably go and set up home nearby. You can also buy ant powder, but as this can affect your pets by making them sick if they inhale the powder, I wouldn't recommend it. This actually did happen to one of my dogs and it took me a while to realise the cause of his sickness.

Ants can sometimes undermine the roots of plants, but this is not too much of a problem in most gardens, so generally speaking they can be left alone.

Tip

If you place a flowerpot upside down over an ants' nest, they will quickly fill it with eggs – to help warm them for hatching – and you can just put these eggs on to the bird table – the birds will love them!

Cats

It can be very difficult if a neighbour's cat continues to foul your garden. I do understand this problem as I have two cats myself, one of whom won't leave the garden, so I now set aside a small area of soil, tucked out of sight, freshly turned over for her. But here are just a few other suggestions on damage limitation:

Thomas, my cat, having a snooze

- Keep your soil covered – if you have plants close together this will generally keep cats away;
- If soil is exposed, have short sharp twigs sticking up out of the soil, or cover the soil with holly leaves;
- Scatter the area with used teabags sprinkled with a strong smelling oil such as eucalyptus or citronella – cats don't like it;
- You can buy cat deterrents, such as pepper dust and lion dung pellets, but I'm not too sure how successful they are, but are probably worth a try.

This was never intended to be an exhaustive list of garden pests, and they will vary from region to region, but the information above should give you a few ideas on how best to cope.

Similarly, there are too many plant diseases to list them all here, but many are caused by fungi, and others by bacteria and viruses.

Some plants are more susceptible, for example, roses tend to get black spot, mildew and rust (all fungi). Hollyhocks (*alcea*) are also prone to rust. These conditions seem to be made worse by a damp environment. Sweet peas suffer from powdery mildew but this is often due to a lack of regular watering.

However, any good illustrated gardening book will give you more information about identifying the causes of pest damage and plant diseases, and will also provide details on how best to deal with them. If you are still unsure, take a sample of the diseased plant to your local nursery or horticultural club, who will be only too happy to help you.

And now on the positive side, we move on to the gardeners' friends who will help you in the battle against the enemies.

Who are they and how do you encourage them to visit and stay?

Birds

As I mentioned earlier, birds are wonderful at protecting your plants against aphids, apart from being such a joy to watch. Attract them into the garden by putting up bird feeders – it may take a few weeks for the birds to get used to them, but once they have accepted them, they will tell all their friends. Here are a some tips on how to set up feeders:

- Site the feeders near to trees or shrubs, if you can, as this enables them to quickly escape predators;

- Give them peanuts (but only in special peanut feeders), seeds, and fat during the winter. Birds will need feeding all year round, though they will eat less in the summer after the baby birds have fledged;

- During spring and summer, when birds have newly hatched young to feed, putting out mealworms, which are full of protein, is beneficial for the youngsters. Either buy them live from a good pet shop or, if you can't face dealing with wriggly worms, you can also buy dried mealworms, which are easy to rehydrate.

You can also put up nest boxes – there are different styles to suit different birds; and perhaps grow plants that have berries, which the birds will love in the autumn, cotoneasters for example.

Birds will also need water, not only for drinking but also for bathing to help keep their feathers in tip-top condition. There is nothing so wonderful as seeing a flock of sparrows or perhaps a couple of blackbirds having a real splash around in a bird bath.

And it doesn't have to be an expensive bird bath: I have a plastic pot saucer on my balcony and an old water bowl that the dogs used to use on the patio, and both are now enjoyed by the birds. Just make sure that it is kept topped up with water as the birds will get used to using it and will turn up regularly.

Tip

Put a couple of copper coins into the bird bath to prevent green slime forming.

Small mammals

Hedgehogs are nocturnal, and are to be encouraged as

they will spend the night searching out and eating slugs and snails. If you put a saucer of cat food out each evening, you may well attract a hedgehog, who  will then start turning up regularly and finding his supper in your garden.

Do **NOT** feed hedgehogs bread and milk, as this will make them ill.

A pond is guaranteed to attract frogs and toads, who love nothing better than eating your slugs. And you don't need a country estate to have one – I know of a woman who simply sunk a baby bath into the ground. As long as there is a shallow sloping edge (or perhaps a plank of wood to act as a ramp) on one side for animals to be able to get out easily, it really doesn't have to be very large to attract wildlife – though the water in a smaller pond will evaporate more quickly and you would need to check this regularly. If you have a fish-pond, however, you won't get frogs, as the fish will eat the frogspawn.

82

Insects

An insect is certainly not automatically an enemy, though generally speaking we humans are not that keen on them. There is a saying that if an insect moves slowly, it eats plants; but if it moves fast, it eats other insects.

Here are some of our insect friends.

Bees

So many of our plants, including vegetables, rely on bees for pollination, but recently their numbers have declined dramatically, so everything we can do help them, by providing nectar-rich plants, is to be encouraged. The nectar feeds the adult bees, and pollen feeds the youngsters. Single-flowered plants, not double flowers, are preferred by bees, largely because single flowers give easier access for the bees, but there are some double flowers that are sterile.

Ground beetles

Beetles feed on slugs and soil pests. They are shiny and usually black, move pretty fast and have two separate antennae, distinguishing them from vine weevils (an enemy), who are slow moving, brownish colour and their antennae are connected making them Y-shaped.

Ladybirds

These insects are instantly recognisable, and they love aphids, as do their larvae, whom many people unfortunately fail to recognise. The larvae are bigger than the adult ladybird, are dark grey-blue with yellowish spots, so be aware and please don't squash them.

Worms

Worms are not the most glamorous creatures, but very definitely a gardener's friend. They help enrich the soil by dragging compost from the surface down into the ground, and they also aerate the soil. Don't worry about worm casts on your lawn; just brush them away when they're dry.

Other beneficial species include garden spiders, hover flies (they look like wasps but don't sting) and centipedes (brown and fast moving, whereas millipedes are black, move slowly and eat plants).

There's really not the space to give details of all the beneficial insects you are likely to come across, for there are far too many, but if you are interested, a book on insects is worth having and will certainly help with identification.

It's good to know that many companies that sell bird feeders and birdseed also sell 'homes' for small mammals and insects so, for example, you can get hedgehog houses, and ladybird hotels. Or how about leaving a small corner of your garden especially for them with a pile of logs left to rot down and mounds of leaf litter? This will help them to live out the winter in safety and be ready to start work on your pests come the spring.

Abelia, flowering in late summer

Chapter 5

Growing from Seed

For those of you who are starting to get the 'gardening bug', and have the space and time, growing your own plants from seed can be the most exciting and worthwhile gardening activity. And of course it is a really inexpensive way to grow the number of plants you need for your garden or containers. I found one of the easiest  seeds to grow is verbena bonariensis, shown above, a tall, elegant plant, with long-lasting flowers.

At this stage, I'm only going to cover sowing seeds indoors, as this is definitely less trouble than sowing outdoors, and is much more under your control. Any setbacks can easily discourage you.

Although your ultimate aim will be to collect seed from your own plants (and I will cover this later in this chapter), I want to start by just focusing on growing seeds from packets purchased at a garden centre. These packets will have a picture on the front and growing instructions on the reverse, including germination time and the best time of year to sow. The instructions are important so do keep the packet safe even if you have used all the seeds.

Alternatively, you can order seeds from specialist catalogues but these tend to have no pictures and no instructions – you would then have to find out this information from a plant encyclopaedia. I would not recommend this if you are new to growing from seed as the last thing you want is for the seeds to fail to grow – this can put you off from ever trying again, and that would really be a pity as it truly is a satisfying experience.

What a seed needs

A seed has its own initial supply of nutrients stored within the outer casing. What we have to supply, to bring it to life, is warmth, moisture and air. You can buy special seed compost, but it is not really necessary and any good quality multi-purpose compost will be equally effective.

Seeds come in all shapes and sizes, and by far the easiest to deal with when you're starting out are the larger seeds, for example, sunflower, nasturtium and sweet pea. You can see what you're doing and the seedlings that emerge are not too tiny that they are difficult to handle.

Some seeds have special requirements:

- Hardy geraniums, after the seeds have been sown, need 2–3 weeks in the refrigerator to encourage germination;
- Sweet peas need to be soaked for a few hours to soften the hard outer casing;
- Very small seeds need to be sown on the surface of the compost;
- Larger seeds need to be lightly covered with compost;
- Some seeds will only germinate in the dark.

As you can see, it is important that you follow the instructions on the packet carefully to get the best results.

Tip

One of the easiest ways to start out growing from seed is to grow herbs from seed in pots on your windowsill. This can be done all year round and gives a continuous supply of your favourite herbs.

Equipment you will need

You will need very little in the way of special equipment to get started, but if you are keen on growing your plants from seed, you can always add further equipment, say, a heated propagator, as you need it. The basic requirements are:

- Clean pots or seed trays, with drainage holes and not too flimsy;
- Seed compost or multi-purpose compost;
- Clear plastic bags or cling film or propagator (a seed tray with a clear plastic lid and air vents);
- Vermiculite – can be used instead of compost to give the seeds a light covering;
- Dibber or pencil for making little planting holes;
- Widger or teaspoon for lifting seedlings;
- Small watering can with fine rose;
- Plant labels – white plastic ones are cheap and if you write in pencil, they can be re-used.

Sowing seed

How do you start and what do you do? Gather all your equipment together in a clean and clutter free space, and follow these instructions:

- Fill your pots or seed trays with the compost to about ½ inch (1 cm) below the rim;
- Water the compost well;
- For smaller seeds, tip the seeds into the palm of your hand, then lightly tap it with your other hand to sprinkle the seeds thinly on to the compost;

- For large seeds, just gently push the seed into the compost until it is just covered by its own depth of compost;
- Cover the seeds thinly with vermiculite or compost if required – for very fine seeds, do not cover with compost, but stretch cling film over the pot;
- Clearly write the plant name and date planted on a plant label, and push it into the compost in the side of the pot or tray;
- Seal the pots or trays inside a large loose plastic bag or propagator;
- Place them in a warm, light place – a bright window sill is ideal but out of direct sunlight;
- Check on them each day: if the compost starts to dry out – the compost turns a lighter colour – then you can either water gently using a small watering can with a fine rose, but be careful not to damage any emerging seedlings. Or what I prefer to do is to stand the pots in water until the compost darkens again.

Tip

Instead of plastic plant pots, you can use old yoghurt pots, just punch a few holes in the bottom, cardboard toilet rolls, coffee cup sleeves, and even newspaper, as a cheaper alternative for growing seeds.

Emerging seedlings

Germination and potting on

When the seeds start to germinate, the first thing you will see growing are the seed leaves – two small, often round, leaves that look very much the same on all plants. Then the true leaves appear and you can recognise that these leaves are more like those on the mature plant.

It is at this stage, when the true leaves appear, that the seedlings are ready for pricking out, which is gardener-speak for transplanting them out into new pots. Don't leave it too long after the first true leaves appear, as the seedlings will grow spindly and prone to collapse.

So how do you do this?

- Fill clean 3½ inch (9 cm) pots or seed trays with seed or multi-purpose compost and firm it down – tapping the pot on the bench also helps to remove any air pockets;

- Gently loosen each seedling from its compost with a widger or the handle of a teaspoon, holding the seedling by its seed leaf, not by its stem, which is very fragile and easily damaged;

- Make a hole in the new compost with a dibber or pencil and gently lower the seedling into the hole, making sure that all the roots are tucked into the hole and the seed leaves are just above the surface;

- Carefully fill the hole to cover the roots;

- Space the seedlings in a seed tray about 1½–2 inches (3.5–4 cms) apart, otherwise plant them in-dividually into 3½ inch (9 cm) pots;

- Any weak seedlings or those you don't think you will need can go into the compost bin;

- Water carefully, either by soaking the tray or pot, or using a small watering can with a fine rose;

- Place in bright light, but not direct sunlight, and check regularly;

- Keep moist, but not too wet as the seedlings will rot;

- Once the seedlings have grown into bushy little plants and their roots fill the pots or trays, then it is time to plant them either into your containers in the garden or into the garden border, once all risk of frost has passed;

- You can now start to feed them with a general-purpose fertiliser, following the instructions on the packet.

That's all there is to it!

It's not as complicated as you might think, but it does require a little thought and care – the equipment must be clean to prevent disease or infection; don't over-water; provide enough light; handle gently; and check them regularly.

You can feel immensely proud of yourself when you tell all your friends that you grew these beautiful plants from seed yourself – it's a feeling that never really goes away.

Collecting your own seeds

For me, collecting seeds from my own plants (or my neighbours' and friends' plants), is one of the most exciting and rewarding methods of getting new plants for free. Yes, nature does this herself each year, but by collecting these seeds myself, I can make sure the plants are exactly where I want them, either in the borders or in pots.

I am going to look at the easy to find and easy to collect plants, which will give you great confidence in your abilities and encourage you to search out and tackle more challenging plants.

Poppy seed heads

The equipment you need is as basic as a pair of scissors, brown paper bags (certainly not plastic, or if you don't have paper bags, envelopes would do as well) and a pen for labelling the bags. Believe me, you need to label the bags straight away with the name of the plant and the date collected, as you will forget what is in there: mind you, it can be interesting to sow un-named seeds and watch what plants appear!

Among the easiest seeds to collect for a beginner are: Poppies, Aquilegias, Nasturtiums, Marigolds, Honesty, Foxgloves, Sunflowers, Pansies or Violas, Sweet

Peas, Cosmos and Love-in-a Mist. And there are just a few simple steps to follow:

- After flowering, leave the flowers on the plant – don't dead-head;
- Allow the seed head to dry as much as possible on the plant – there comes a point when you may have to check your plants daily to keep an eye on what is happening – and wait until the head or pod looks as if it is about to split open;
- Choose a day that is dry with little wind, and find a plant that looks healthy and free of pests;
- Carefully cut the stem a few inches below the seed-head and pop into one of your paper bags, close and label immediately;
- Store the bags somewhere dry, and check regularly to see whether the seed heads have opened;
- Once open, shake the seeds out on to clean paper and remove any remaining bits of seed head;
- Now store the seeds in a sealed paper bag or envelope, label and keep in a cool, dry place until ready to use.

Why not start a seed swap project in your own community, a fantastic way to increase your stock of plants for free?

Chapter 6

Organic Gardening

Awareness of organic gardening has been growing over the past few years and I want to just take a moment in this chapter to explore some of the reasons for going organic as well as how to get started.

Organic gardening, as little as some 25 years ago, was considered a slightly eccentric way of gardening, a little bit 'hippy' and mainly for those with the time or money to devote to it. Yet for many hundreds of years previously, farmers grew crops for food using just the resources provided by Mother Nature.

And it is only recently, with the increasing demands for cheap food, that farmers, and subsequently gardeners, have turned to using synthetic chemicals to protect their crops. So why should we gardeners take any interest in this?

The dangers of chemicals

Synthetic chemicals are all around us, in our clothes, our beauty products, and the contents of our homes, and we would certainly struggle to achieve the standards of living we would like without them.

But they are also in our food, much of which is produced using chemical fertilisers. The producer can achieve much higher yields of his crop and consequently larger returns. The downside of this, however, is that although these fertilisers provide, in the short term, a quick-acting booster for the plants, in the longer term, they can have a devastating effect on the fertility of the soil and cause the destruction of beneficial soil organisms including earthworms.

There is also evidence that these fertilisers can alter the vitamin and mineral contents of some crops. And chemical fertilisers can inevitably find their way into the water supply, with no guarantees that all the chemicals are removed during the filtration process.

Synthetic chemicals are also used to protect our crops from pests and diseases in the form of insecticides and herbicides – the first for controlling insect pests and the second for controlling weeds. But more and more studies are now confirming that these are dangerous to humans in terms of reduced immune system function, and links to cancer. The World Health Organisation estimates that there are over one million cases of pesticide poisoning every year (www.who.int).

Pesticides also affect the environment, damaging ecosystems and resulting in the loss of native beneficial species. In addition, the continued use of herbicides can result in resistance, causing the targeted plant species to develop immunity.

Because of the spectacular short-term 'improvements' in the growth of plants, it is not surprising that many gardeners took up the use of synthetic fertilisers and pesticides in their own gardens.

It is becoming more and more clear, however, that we gardeners are in a position to take the lead to reduce the impact caused to the environment – if every single gardener took just a few small steps towards organic gardening, think of the benefits that would accrue to wildlife and the environment.

So what is organic gardening?

Organic gardening is much more than just not using synthetic chemicals in the form of fertilisers and pesticides in your garden. An organic gardener thinks of the garden and its plants as being part of a whole system within nature. An organic gardener will work in harmony with nature and aims to continually replenish any resources the garden consumes.

The RHS describes organic gardening as:

A fundamental feature is reliance on manures and fertilisers derived only from animal or plant remains. These are practical elements of a broader philosophy, which takes a holistic view of gardening, emphasising the interdependence of life forms. Conserving natural resources and avoiding pollution and health hazards are further important elements in the concept of organic gardening.

(www.rhs.org.uk/Gardening/Sustainable-
gardening/pdfs/c_and_e_organic)

This holistic view of gardening takes into account not just the immediate plants in the garden but also considers the effects of gardening on the wider environment by focusing on developing a healthy and fertile soil.

Now this sounds all very grand, but how can a new gardener get to grips with this concept and actually put it into practice?

Practical steps to organic gardening

Earlier in the book, in Chapter 4, I have already covered a few ways that a gardener can start using natural methods to deter pests and weeds, for example, encouraging birds into the garden to eat aphids and using mulch to suppress weeds. But here are a few more ideas that can help.

Soil fertility

Soil fertility is important in that it provides your plants with the essential nutrients they need to provide strong healthy growth: and a strong healthy plant is much more likely to resist disease and shrug off pests.

Incorporating organic matter into the soil in the form of garden compost is crucially important, and the earlier you can get your compost bin in place and start making compost, the better (see Chapter 1 on what you can and cannot compost). The compost can either be dug into the soil in either autumn or spring, or alternatively can be laid as a thick mulch, which is then incorporated into the soil over time by the gardener's friend, the earthworm.

If you have access to, and want to use, farm manure, then just make sure it is well rotted before putting it on to your garden as it is quite strong and can 'burn' plants. A better idea is to incorporate it into your compost bin, or leave it to rot down for around six months or so before using as a mulch.

An alternative, if you have the space, say in a vegetable plot, is to plant 'green manures', which are grown over the winter and then dug into the soil before they set seed. This picture shows green manures sown on a grand scale: a field of phacelia, which has pretty blue flowers. The seeds are readily available from seed  merchants and you can choose from mustard, phacelia, clovers, or winter field beans, which will also give you a crop of beans for the kitchen!

Fertilisers

Chemical fertilisers, as mentioned above, can certainly bring instant results in terms of more vigorous growth and bigger and better flowers. But there are organic alternatives

You can buy organic fertilisers in the form of process-dried manures. There are different types, for example, fish, blood and bone meal, which provide nitrogen, or wood ash which supplies phosphorus. All of the different combinations, suitable for different purposes can all be purchased from your local garden centre.

Or it is quite easy to make your own fertiliser, and here are a few suggestions:

- Mix chopped banana peel, ground egg shells and coffee grounds, and fork into the soil around your plants – banana peel is especially appreciated by roses!

- If you have a clump of nettles in your garden, then why not make a liquid feed to fertilise your plants? Soak crushed nettles in water for about a month; strain and dilute the feed one part in ten and spray on to your plants – the liquid should be pale amber in colour. It can also act as a fungicide. The strained nettles can be added to the compost heap.

- If you have a fish tank, use the old water from the tank to water your plants.

- Combine one tablespoon of Epsom salts with one gallon of water in a watering can. Use this about once a month.

- Eggs shells can either be ground up and dried, then sprinkled around plants in the garden, or alternatively soak the shells in water, letting them sit for about four weeks, then dilute one cup of the egg shell water in one gallon of plain water to fertilise your plants.

I hope that has given you a few ideas you can use as an alternative to chemical fertilisers, and if you search online, you will probably find a lot more.

Pest control

An excellent way of controlling garden pests is by using biological controls. Supplied by mail order, these predators and parasites, are used to kill off such pests as slugs, vine weevils and chafer grubs, as well as in the greenhouse for pests, such as, aphids and red spider mites.

The control arrives in small, sealed packets, which need to be kept in the fridge until you are ready to use, and then it is simply sprinkled into the watering can. It is best to use these at the start of the growing season, in spring.

Plant breeders are now breeding new cultivars that are more resistant to disease, and gardeners are able to find, for example, blight resistant potatoes, as well as for the flower garden, rust resistant hollyhocks. It is worth browsing the seed catalogues to find these new cultivars.

Water conservation

Part of seeing organic gardening as a way of contributing to the wider environment is to consider what we can do to save water, a finite resource and one we need to look after. To conserve water, you can install a water butt, or rain catchment system, to collect the rainwater off your roof and gutters and use this to water your plants. In fact, most plants prefer rainwater to tap water.

Another option is to use 'grey' water, in other words, left over bath water – just fill a couple of buckets to use for watering pot plants and hanging baskets. You can now get a whole 'greywater' system to take all the waste water from your bathroom, washing machine and dishwasher to use for irrigation in the garden, although you would have to be aware of what chemicals you are using in washing powders and not to put bleach down the drains.

If you only have a tiny space, then a couple of buckets left out in the garden or yard, will collect rainwater as well. This is what I do on my balcony, which saves me carrying a heavy watering can from the bathroom tap.

Recycling

I have already touched on making garden compost in Chapter 1, but if you are unable, through lack of space, to compost, you may find that your local council provides a facility for collecting green waste (and in some areas, I understand, food waste).

But recycling of course, can also involve making use of all kinds of materials in your garden, and here are a few ideas:

- Use upside-down wine bottles to create an edging for a path or border – drink the wine first!

- Used wooden lollypop sticks made great plant labels;

- Any sort of container can be turned into plant pots, including old boots, tin cans, saucepans, colanders (especially good for alpines that need good drainage), olive oil cans.

- Tyres make great plant containers and are particular good for growing potatoes: plant the seed potatoes in the first tyre and as the plants grow, you can add the next tyre and top up with compost;

- Old carpet or cardboard can be laid as a weed suppressant and covered in gravel;

- Pallets can be recycled into fencing, compost bins, potting benches and even plant stands;
- Use plastic drink bottles, cut in half, as individual cloches for seedlings.

Before you throw anything away, just think for a minute if it could have a further use.

What can you do?

I have barely skimmed the surface of organic gardening in this chapter, but I hope that I have given you an idea of what is involved and that, actually, it doesn't have to be that complicated. Of course, you don't have to do everything all at once. Just take one aspect of organic gardening that you feel you can do and start with that.

But if you want to be sure that the vegetables you pick from your garden and put on your plate are completely chemical free, and if you feel it is important to protect beneficial insects and wildlife, then it is certainly worth doing.

If you want to find out more, there are plenty of resources available to help you (see the Further Reading and Websites of Interest sections).

Conclusion

I hope that this book has been of some help to you. The most important thing to remember is not to get too serious about it all. Gardening is supposed to be fun, so relax. And if you have a stressful job, then just getting out in the garden or back yard amongst plants is one of the best ways to unwind.

Don't be apprehensive about your garden, and just give it as much time as you can. Don't get too hung up about whether you are doing it right or wrong – it really doesn't matter too much, it's your garden. Do what you enjoy most, and the chances are that it will go right.

Remember that plants want to grow and multiply, so unless you do something horribly wrong, they will probably survive and prosper. And this book is here to help prevent that 'horribly wrong' from happening.

As I said in the Introduction, my aim in writing this book was to motivate, inspire and encourage you to take the first steps in gardening – I do hope that I have done this.

Enjoy!

Geranium 'Rozanne'

Appendix I

Single Digging Technique

If you are making a new garden bed or border, or if you have a vegetable plot, then it is important to dig the ground before planting – it improves the structure of the soil. If the soil is too compacted, the roots are not able to make a way into the soil, and grow.

These are the basic tools you will need:

- sharp spade,
- fork,
- compost,
- wheelbarrow (if you have a large plot to dig, this can be helpful).

And just follow these steps:

- Clean out any weeds or stones on the surface;
- Work in a straight line along the shortest edge of the border and then work backwards, so you are facing the area you have already dug;
- Push the spade down vertically into the soil, lift the soil and throw it forward creating a trench – pull out any weeds as you go;

109

- Put this soil from your first trench into a heap near to the other end of the plot;

- Cover the bottom of the trench with a layer of compost – 2–3 inches (5–8 cms) should be fine, more if you have really thick clay soil;

- Dig a second trench next to the first and throw this soil forward into the first trench – try and flick it over so that it lands upside down;

- Cover the bottom of this trench with compost as before, and move on to the next;

- Continue like this until you get to the end, then fill up the last trench with the soil from the first trench that you put aside at the beginning.

And that's it. In most circumstances you will only need to do this once. From then on, all you need to do is to put a thick layer of compost over the ground and the worms will mix it up into the existing soil for you. If you have a large area to dig, do it in stages, don't try and do it all at once – your back won't thank you for it.

Appendix II

Main Tasks for the Four Seasons

This will give you a checklist of the major tasks to be done in the garden at the appropriate time of year. I can't be too precise about the timing as it very much depends on the climate where you live, so I've listed the tasks by season instead of by month. Hopefully this will provide easy-to-follow guidelines for you.

Spring

- Scatter fertiliser around roses and shrubs and fork in;
- Mulch borders;
- Plant new border perennials;
- Stake any plants now that will grow tall during the summer;
- Dead-head early flowering bulbs, but don't remove the leaves;
- Prune spring-flowering shrubs;

- Sow seeds indoors – annual and perennial flowers, and vegetables;
- Start keeping weeds under control now;
- Start to cut the lawn.

Summer

- Dead-head roses as the flowers fade;
- Plant out tender annuals, containers and put up hanging baskets;
- Water containers daily and feed once a week;
- Cut the lawn once a week;
- Clip hedges;
- Cut back the flower stems of herbaceous perennials as they fade;
- Carry on weeding.

Autumn

- Plant spring-flowering bulbs;
- Clear away summer bedding plants;
- Clip hedges;
- Rake up fallen leaves from lawns and borders;
- Any tender plants in pots should be brought in under cover;
- Protect tender plants in borders by covering with straw or bracken;

- Plant out new perennial plants;
- Dig up, divide and replace herbaceous perennials;
- Dig over new borders;
- Put a layer of mulch on to borders, after weeding and watering..

Winter

- Plant garlic cloves mid-December for harvesting mid-July;
- Provide food and water for birds;
- Clean all tools and wash spare pots and seed trays;
- Clear any snow from the branches of evergreen trees and shrubs;
- Check fences, paths etc. for any repairs that are needed;
- Look through seed and plant catalogues;
- Look at your garden photos and make plans for the following year.

Crocosmia 'Lucifer' on a sunny summer's day

Glossary

Acid (soil) With a *pH* value of less than 7 – necessary for growing camellias, heathers and rhododendrons (acid-loving plants).

Alkaline (soil) With a *pH* value greater than 7.

Alpine A term applied to a small plant grown in a rock garden, originating from high mountain regions.

Annual A plant that grows, flowers, sets seed and dies within one growing season.

Bedding A term used to describe plants used in temporary summer displays in the garden.

Biennial A plant that grows and produces leaves in the first season, flowers, sets seed and dies in the second.

Broadcast sowing Scattering seeds randomly over a border as opposed to sowing in straight rows (*drills*).

Bulb The underground storage organ of a group of plants, such as the daffodil.

Compost a) *Organic* material obtained by the decomposition of plant matter, used as a soil improver or *mulch*.

115

b)   Mixture of ingredients used for growing plants in containers, purchased in bags from the garden centre.

Conifer   A tree that bears cones.

Corm   Similar to a *bulb*, the underground storage organ of plants such as crocus and cyclamen.

Crocks   Refers to broken clay flowerpots, used to cover the base of containers to provide good drainage.

Deadhead   To remove faded flowers to prevent self-seeding and encourage new flowers.

Deciduous   Plants that lose their leaves for winter.

Dibber   Tool used to make small planting holes for seedlings.

Drill   A straight, shallow depression in the soil for sowing seeds.

Ericaceous compost   Potting *compost* used specifically for acid-loving plants, such as, camellias.

Evergreen   Plants that retain their leaves all year round.

Germination   Is the first stage in the growth of a seed, when the roots emerge and the *seed leaves* appear.

Half-hardy   Plants that can be grown outside on-ly after the last frosts of spring.

Hardy   Plants able to survive outside all year round.

Herbaceous   Plants that die back to ground level in winter.

Humus   Decayed *organic* matter.

Inorganic   A synthetic chemical compound.

Leaf-mould   Decayed leaf matter, good for soil enrichment.

Loam   Thought of as the perfect soil con-sisting of a mixture of clay, *humus* and sand.

Manure   Usually stable manure – a mixture of dung and straw bedding, which must be stored for several months to rot down before it is ready to use on the soil.

Mulch   A covering, either home-made *com-post* to improve the soil, or bark, gravel or membrane to suppress weeds and preserve moisture.

Neutral (soil)   A *pH* value of 7 – the ideal to grow most plants is 6 or 6.5.

Node   Refers to a leaf joint on the stem of the plant.

Organic   Describes a method of gardening, which does not allow the use of syn-

117

thetic chemicals or fertilisers. It also refers to anything containing carbon – animal or plant material.

Perennial	A plant that can live for many years.
pH	Measures the amount of lime in the soil on a scale of 0–14.
Pinch out	To remove a growing shoot to encourage side shoots and a more bushy plant.
Pricking out	Moving seedlings into another pot or tray to give them more space to grow on.
Potting on	This simply means moving a plant into a larger container.
Rhizome	The creeping underground storage organ of plants such as bearded iris.
Runner	A stem that roots where it touches the soil to produce more plants such as strawberries.
Seed leaves	The first leaves, usually round, to appear when seeds germinate.
Tender	Refers to a plant that will be damaged or killed by frost.
Tuber	The underground storage organ for plants such as dahlia.
Variegated	A plant having leaves of more than one colour.

Further Reading

Reader's Digest New Encyclopedia of Garden Plants and Flowers (Reader's Digest Association, 2003) – this is a comprehensive guide to plants with essential information about cultivation and photographs of each plant. I highly recommend it.

The Royal Horticultural Society Gardening Manual (Dorling Kindersley, 2000) – is a complete manual on how to plan, create, and maintain your garden. However, this book does assume a certain amount of knowledge.

I have found the following three books extremely helpful, reflecting the different approach and personality of their authors, and they are available on Amazon:

The Weekend Gardener, Monty Don (Bloomsbury Publishing plc, 1995).

Geoff Hamilton's Cottage Gardens, Geoff Hamilton (BBC Worldwide Ltd, 1995).

How to be a Gardener, Book One, Alan Titchmarsh (BBC Worldwide Ltd, 2002).

And these two books are simply gorgeous to look at, and again both available on Amazon:

The Garden: a Year at Home Farm, Dan Pearson (BBC Worldwide Ltd, 2001), (this book is sub-titled *a Year at Home Garden* in the USA).

Colour for Adventurous Gardeners, Christopher Lloyd (BBC Worldwide Ltd, 2001).

Websites of Interest

The websites that I have found most useful are:

http://www.rhs.org.uk/ – the website of the Royal Horticultural Society and a mine of information.

http://www.bbc.co.uk/gardening – this is great site to find gardening information, and there are message forums available if you need help with a specific problem.

http://www.greengardener.co.uk – this site specialises in organic gardening, selling organic biological controls for garden pests, as well as giving advice.

http://www.gardenorganic.org.uk – the UK's leading growing organic charity

Picture Credits

Images used under the Creative Commons license:

Page 5: bare soil, Bryn Pinzgauer from Flickr;

Page 9: soil testing, omaniblog from Flickr

Page 12: compost bins, dsa66503 from Flickr

Page 26: gravel garden, sarahgardenvisit from Flickr

Page 28: plant nursery, tracie7779 from Flickr

Page 43: lavender , Linda N. from Flickr

Page 56: schizostylis peganum, from Flickr

Page 57: hellebore, amdougherty from Flickr

Page 69: slug damage, Chris Penny from Flickr

Page 74: large cabbage white caterpillars, Ricky Cosmos
   from Flickr:

Page 76: vine weevil, davidshort from Flickr

Page 82: European hedgehog; © Soil-Net,
   http://www.soil-net.com, Cranfield University,
   UK, 2012

Page 92: seedlings, briannaorg from Flickr

Page 95: poppy seed heads, hughrocks from Flickr

Page 101: green manures, karenandkerry from Flickr

Page 105: potato tyre planter, photo can be seen at:
   http://www.real-sonic-bloom.com/organic_
   gardening/ growing_ potatoes_in_a_ tire_
   planter.htm

Images in the public domain:

Page 65: dandelion, botanical colour plate from *Flora Londinensis*, 1777–98, drawn by William Kilburn.

All other pictures are from the author's own garden.

About the Author

Fran Barnwell (the pen name of author Linda McGrory) has been providing gardening advice for beginners for many years through her website:
http://www.newtogardening.co.uk.

Fran's philosophy is to provide simple and straightforward advice for anyone starting out with gardening, whether that is indoors or outdoors, with a good-sized garden or just a window ledge.

First published in 2005, *How to Start Gardening: A Step by Step Guide for Beginners (2nd edition)* is the first book in The New to Gardening Series. The second book in the series, *How to Grow Orchids: A Beginner's Guide to Growing Orchids*, was published in June 2012 and is available on Amazon in both the US and UK:
http://www.amazon.com/dp/B008EM5CZ4
http://www.amazon.co.uk/dp/B008EM5CZ4

2717776R00069

Printed in Great Britain
by Amazon.co.uk, Ltd.,
Marston Gate.